MW00895466

Nita Mehta's
Vegetarian
SoupS

Vegetarian

100% TRIED & TESTED RECIPES

Nita Mehta

B.Sc. (Home Science), M.Sc. (Food and Nutrition) Gold Medalist

Tanya Mehta

PUBLISHERS PVT LTD

Nita Mehta's
Vegetarian
SoupS

© Copyright 2004 **SNAB** Publishers Pvt Ltd

WORLD RIGHTS RESERVED. The contents—all recipes, photographs and drawings are original and copyrighted. No portion of this book shall be reproduced, stored in a retrieval system or transmitted by any means, electronic, mechanical, photocopying, recording or otherwise, without the written permission of the publishers.

While every precaution is taken in the preparation of this book, the publisher and the author assume no responsibility for errors or omissions. Neither is any liability assumed for damages resulting from the use of information contained herein.

TRADEMARKS ACKNOWLEDGED. Trademarks used, if any, are acknowledged as trademarks of their respective owners. These are used as reference only and no trademark infringement is intended upon. Ajinomoto (monosodium glutamade, MSG) is a trademark of Aji-no-moto company of Japan. Use it sparingly if you must as a flavour enhancer.

First Edition 2004
ISBN 81-7869-084-5

Food Styling and Photography: **SNAB**

Layout and laser typesetting :

National Information
Technology Academy
3A/3, Asaf Ali Road
New Delhi-110002
☏ 23252948

Published by :

Publishers Pvt. Ltd.
3A/3 Asaf Ali Road,
New Delhi - 110002
Tel: 23252948, 23250091
Telefax:91-11-23250091

Editorial and Marketing office:
E-159, Greater Kailash-II, N.Delhi-48
Fax: 91-11-29225218, 29229558
Tel: 91-11-29214011, 29218727, 29218574
E-Mail: nitamehta@email.com
☐ snab@snabindia.com
Website: http://www.nitamehta.com
Website: http://www.snabindia.com

Distributed by :
THE VARIETY BOOK DEPOT
A.V.G. Bhavan, M 3 Con Circus,
New Delhi - 110 001
Tel : 23417175, 23412567; Fax : 23415335
Email: varietybookdepot@rediffmail.com

Printed by :
AJANTA OFFSET & PACKAGING LTD

Rs. 89/-

INTRODUCTION

Soups are heart warmers which cheer you up. A good soup should be pleasing and natural without any artificial colours and free from greasiness. The flavour should be full and good, not overpowering. Too much garlic or spices should be avoided. Generally soups are served before the main meals and care should be taken that these soups should be light enough to be served as appetizers. However, there are some heavy or substantial soups which can make a complete meal with some bread.

Soups may be very thin and clear, like the Tom Yum Thai soup, or slightly thickened by using cornflour as in Chinese soups or the vegetable itself is pureed to give the desired consistency, as in mushroom soup. There are Indian soups/shorbas like rasam, classic Continental soups like cream of tomato or cream of vegetable and other International soups like minestrone of Italy or the French onion soup of France.

Enjoy your meal with a hot bowl of appetizing soup!

ABOUT THE RECIPES
WHAT'S IN A CUP?
INDIAN CUP
1 teacup = 200 ml liquid
AMERICAN CUP
1 cup = 240 ml liquid (8 oz.)
The recipes in this book were tested with the Indian teacup which holds 200 ml liquid.

CONTENTS

CHINESE & THAI SOUPS   43

Soup Accompaniments

Picture of all accompaniments on page 2

Accompaniments are served separately or on the side in the soup plate. I prefer serving croutons separately, as they usually turn soggy by the time one actually starts with the soup! Soup sticks can be made more interesting if warmed and served in a tall glass. To warm them, heat in the oven for 5 minutes.

Garlic Bread Fingers - Take a broad french loaf, cut into half lengthwise. Mix 3 tbsp softened butter with ½ tsp garlic paste, ¾ tsp each of red chilli flakes and oregano. Spread the butter on the cut surface. Cut into ¾" thick fingers. Bake them in an oven at 200°C for 12-15 minutes on the wire rack, till golden and crisp.

Spicy Nachos - Knead 1½ cups maize flour (makki ka atta) and 1 cup flour (maida) with 1 tsp salt, 1 tsp oregano, ½ tsp red chilli flakes and 2 tbsp oil, with enough water to a slightly firm dough. Make marble sized balls and roll out into thin chappatis. Prick it with a fork. Cut into 4 or 8 triangles and deep fry on medium flame till golden. Serve hot. You can make them in advance and store in an air tight container after they cool down.

Cheese Munchys - Take a bread slice and butter both sides of the bread lightly. Top with a cheese slice. Sprinkle 1 tsp of finely chopped capsicum and 1 tsp of finely chopped deseeded tomato. Sprinkle a pinch of freshly crushed pepper and salt. Place on the wire rack of a preheated oven at 200°C for 5-7 minutes, till the bread turns crisp from below. Remove from oven and cut into 4 fingers with a pizza cutter. If you like, cut each finger into half to give 8 small pieces.

Herbed Croutons - Cut 1 day old bread into tiny cubes, about ¼" cubes. Heat oil in a kadhai. Reduce heat. Add bread cubes to the hot oil and remove from oil immediately when they start to change colour, within 1 minute or they will turn extra brown. Immediately sprinkle the hot fried croutons with ¼ tsp pepper or oregano or basil or mixed herbs and a pinch of salt.

Nutty Spread- Toast 1 tsp sesame seeds (til) & 1 tsp chopped walnuts on a tawa on low heat till sesame seeds turn golden. Remove from tawa. Mix 1 tbsp softened butter with 1 tbsp cheese spread. Add toasted sesame seeds and walnuts to it. Add 1-2 tbsp milk to make the spread softer, if it is cold weather. Keep aside till serving time. At serving time, serve cold spread with warm soup sticks.

Soup Garnishes

All garnishes should be done on the soup after it has been heated and put in the soup bowl or cup, just before serving.

- Drop cream on the soup in a circle with a spoon, slowly to get a round swirl
- Grate cheese into thin long shavings on the soup
- Thinly sliced almonds add the crunch as well as eye appeal.
- Very tiny pieces of paneer or capsicum or carrot (diced vegetables)
- Finely chopped greens of a spring onion or coriander or parsley
- Fried Rice noodles - these extremely thin noodles resemble long, translucent white hair. When deep fried they explode dramatically into a tangle of airy, crunchy strands that are used for garnishing soups.

To Prepare Stock for Soups

Fresh Vegetable Stock (makes 6 cups)

1 onion - chopped
1 carrot - chopped
1 potato - chopped
5 french beans - chopped)
½ tsp salt
7 cups water

1. Mix all ingredients and pressure cook to give 1 whistle. Reduce heat and cook for 10-15 minutes on low heat. Remove from fire.
2. Do not mash the vegetables if a clear soup is to be prepared. Strain and use as required or store in refrigerator (freezer compartment) for just about a week.

Tip: Storing the stock for more than a week may let bacteria develop in the stock!

Ready-made Stock (makes 2½ cups) ... Quick Stock

Vegetarian or chicken soup cubes or seasoning cubes may be boiled with water and used instead of fresh stock, if you are short of time. These seasoning cubes are easily available in the market and are equally good in taste.

1 seasoning cube (extra taste), chicken or vegetarian (maggi, knorr or any other brand)
2½ cups of water

1. Crush 1 seasoning cube roughly in a pan.
2. Add 2½ cups of water. Give one boil. Use as required.

Note: The seasoning cube has a lot of salt, so reduce salt if you substitute this stock with the fresh stock. Check taste before adding salt.

Carrot Soup

Serves 4

2 tbsp butter
250 gm carrots - chopped very finely (2 cups)
1 bay leaf (tej patta)
½ tsp salt or to taste
1 tsp pepper, or to taste
2 stock cubes (maggi or knorr) dissolved in 3 cups of water to get stock
croutons of 1-2 bread slices, see page 11

1. Heat 2 tbsp butter in a pan, add chopped carrots and bay leaf. Cook for 4-5 minutes. Add salt and pepper.
2. Add 1 cup of prepared stock (cube+water). Bring to a boil and simmer for 2 minutes. Remove from fire, cool.
3. Churn in a mixer to a puree. Reheat soup and add the remaining stock (2 cups) and give 1 boil. Serve hot garnished with croutons.

Vegetable Cheese Broth
with Cheese Balls

Serves 4-5

1 tbsp butter
1 bay leaf (tej patta)
½ cup finely chopped cauliflower (phool gobhi)
½ cup finely chopped cabbage (bandgobhi)
½ cup finely chopped carrot (gajar)
3-4 french beans - finely chopped
¾ cup milk
3 tbsp level cornflour dissolved in ¼ cup cold milk or water
1½ tsp salt
½ tsp pepper
½ tsp oregano
2 tbsp finely chopped capsicum
10-15 leaves of fresh basil or tender tulsi leaves - finely shredded into thin
long pieces
4 cubes cheese, (cheddar cheese) - grated (¾ cup)

CHEESE BALLS
**½ cup grated paneer, 3 tbsp dry bread crumbs, ¼ tsp pepper,
¼ tsp oregano, ¼ tsp salt, 1 tbsp finely chopped coriander or parsley**

1. Mix all ingredients of cheese balls in a bowl. Make about 8-10 small balls, almost resembling size of a marble. Keep in fridge till serving time.
2. Heat butter in a sauce pan or kadhai, add bay leaf, cauliflower, cabbage, carrot & beans. Saute for 2-3 min.
3. Add 5 cups of water and bring to a boil. Cover and simmer for about 2-3 minutes, till the vegetables are slightly tender.
4. Add milk, dissolved cornflour, salt, pepper, oregano and capsicum. Give 1 boil, check the seasoning.
5. To serve, warm the cheese balls for 1 minute in a microwave or saute in a non-stick frying pan for 2 minutes in 1 tsp butter. Keep aside.
6. Put the soup on fire. Add basil. Cook 1- 2 minutes. Remove soup from fire. Add grated cheese and mix.
7. Pour hot soup in individual bowls, top each with 2 cheese balls and sprinkle with freshly ground pepper. If you like, you can serve the warmed cheese balls on the side, in the soup plate.

Cream of Mushroom

Most of the mushrooms are pureed to give taste and texture to the soup but some are finely chopped and added towards the end for that special bite. Garnished with some greens, this soup is a treat for the mushroom lovers.

Picture on facing Page   *Serves 4-5*

200 gm mushrooms
2 tsp butter, 1 onion - chopped
2 flakes garlic, 1 bay leaf (tej patta)
2 tbsp maida (plain flour)
1 tsp salt, ½ tsp white pepper, 1½ cups milk

TOPPING
2 tbsp cream, some chopped spring onion greens (optional)

1. Roughly chop 150 gm of mushrooms. Finely cut the remaining 50 gm of mushrooms for topping and keep aside.

2. Melt butter in a heavy bottom pan. Add chopped onion, 150 gm roughly chopped mushrooms, garlic

Contd...

and bay leaf. Stir for 3-4 minutes. Do not brown the onions.

3. Add maida and stir for 1 minute. Add 3 cups of water, 1 tsp salt, ½ tsp pepper and bring to a boil. Reduce heat and cook covered for 5 minutes. Remove from heat. Cool.

4. Place mixture in mixer/food processor and grind to a smooth puree. Strain puree through a soup strainer.

5. Put the puree back in the pan. Add milk and finely chopped mushrooms. Boil. Simmer for 2 minutes.

6. Lower heat and add cream and chopped spring onion greens. Mix well and serve hot.

Mushroom & Celery Soup

For Mushroom & Celery Soup, to the above mushroom soup, add 4 tbsp chopped celery stalks at step 2 along with the onion. Proceed in the same way as given above.

◁ *Lettuce Soup: Recipe on page 22*

Lettuce Soup

Picture on page 20   *Serves 4*

A lovely pale green, light textured soup. Surplus lettuce which is not crisp enough for salads can be utilized in a good way!

200-250 gms ice berg lettuce (1 head)
1½ tbsp butter
1 small onion - chopped
¼ tsp black peper, ½ tsp sugar
¼ tsp grated nutmeg (jaiphal)
salt to taste
1 cup milk

1. Separate the lettuce leaves and wash them very well in 2-3 changes of water. Cut them into shreds.
2. Boil 3 cups water with 1 tsp salt. Add the lettuce leaves to the boiling water and cook for 3-5 minutes in salted water. Strain. Keep stock and leaves aside separately.

3. Melt butter in a deep pan or kadhai. Cook the onion till soft, for 1-2 minutes. Keeping aside 2 tbsp lettuce shreds, add the rest to the onion. Stir.

4. Add the stock and bring to a boil.
Add black pepper, sugar and nutmeg. Add salt according to taste. Simmer for 1-2 minutes. Remove from fire.

5. Cool the mixture and blend it in a liquidizer. Strain the soup.

6. Add milk to the soup. Bring to a boil, stirring, and simmer for 1-2 minutes. Serve hot garnished with reserved lettuce shreds.

Fennel Jade Soup

A green coloured broccoli soup. Spinach adds to the nutrition as well as the colour. Carrot and beans give the crunch.

Serves 4

1 cup chopped broccoli (hari gobhi)
1 cup chopped spinach (palak)
1½ tbsp butter
2 tbsp chopped onion
1 small potato - chopped
2 tej patta (bay leaves)
2-3 laung (cloves)
3-4 saboot kali mirch (peppercorns)
½ tsp saunf (fennel seeds)
1 cup milk
2 tbsp carrots - chopped into tiny pieces
2-3 french beans - chopped into tiny pieces
1¼ tsp salt, ¼ tsp white or black pepper
¼ cup cream (optional)

TO GARNISH
2-3 almonds (badam) - chopped finely or a swirl of cream

1. Heat butter in a heavy bottom deep pan. Add chopped onion, potato, tej patta, laung and kali mirch. Saute for 3 minutes.

2. Add saunf.
3. Add broccoli and spinach, cook for 2 minutes.
4. Add 4 cups of water and bring to a boil. Lower heat, cover and cook for 5 minutes. Remove from fire. Cool. Discard the bay leaf and blend in a mixer to a smooth puree. Strain puree through a sieve (chhanni).

5. To the strained soup, add milk, carrots, beans, salt and pepper. Return to fire. Reheat the strained soup. Bring to a boil, stirring continuously.
6. Reduce heat, add cream, mix well. Remove from fire. Do not cook for long, after adding cream.
7. Serve hot topped with a swirl of cream or a few chopped almonds.

French Onion Soup

Picture on page 1   *Serves 3- 4*

3 tbsp butter, 2 onions - sliced very finely
4 flakes garlic - crushed
1 tsp salt to taste, ½ tsp black pepper powder to taste
4 cups stock (given below) or 4 cups water mixed with 2 seasoning
cubes (see page 14)

STOCK
1 carrot - chopped roughly, 1 onion - chopped roughly
2 bay leaves (tej patta), 6-7 peppercorns (saboot kali mirch)
2 laung, 4 cups water, 1 seasoning cube (maggi or knorr)
GARNISHING
25 gm cheddar cheese - grated (use tin or cubes)
½ tsp mustard powder
2 garlic bread slices - toasted or 1 slice of bread - toasted

1. To prepare the stock, pressure cook all ingredients of the stock with 4 cups water to give 3-4 whistles. Strain through a sieve. Keep the clear stock aside.

2. Heat butter in a clean, heavy bottomed pan or kadhai. Fry the onions and garlic over a moderately low heat, stirring occasionally to prevent sticking, until well browned. Do not let the onions burn.

3. Add the stock, stirring continuously. Boil.
4. Add salt, pepper and seasoning cube. Cook on low heat for 5 minutes. Keep soup aside.
5. To garnish the soup, mix the mustard powder and cheese together in a small bowl. Spread over the toasted garlic bread slices or regular bread. Place the toasted slices in the hot oven for 2-3 minutes. Cut each garlic bread into 2 pieces or regular bread into 4 squares.

6. Serve steaming hot soup with one piece of cheese toast floating on top in each serving.

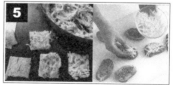

Roasted Eggplant Soup with Mint

Picture on facing page   *Serves 5-6*

500 gms medium aubergine (baigan)
2 tbsp butter
1 small onion - finely chopped
½ cup grated carrot
½ tsp finely chopped garlic
6 cups water, 2 veg seasoning cube (maggi or knorr)
2 tsp lemon juice
1 tbsp finely chopped fresh mint (poodina)
1 tsp salt or to taste, ½ tsp white pepper to taste
fresh mint sprigs, to garnish (optional)

1. Put baigan on a naked flame and roast on all the sides so that the skin gets charred and blackened evenly.

Contd...

Let the baingan be cool enough to handle, then peel and roughly chop.

2. In a large saucepan, melt the butter over medium heat. Add the onion and garlic and cook, stirring occasionally, until golden for about 3-5 minutes.

3. Add the roasted chopped baigan, cook for 8-10 minutes.

4. Add 6 cups water, seasoning cube, 1 tbsp chopped mint, 1 tsp salt, ½ tsp pepper. Give 3-4 boils. Remove from fire. Add lemon juice.

5. Pour into bowls and garnish with grated carrot, a pinch of pepper and with mint sprigs, if desired.

◁ **Basil Tomato Soup : Recipe on page 32**
◁ **Tom Yum : Recipe on page 54**

Basil Tomato Soup

Sweet basil is used to flavour this tomato soup. This basil is different from the holy basil, "Tulsi", which has a hint of bitterness. However, both the basil plants - sweet basil and the holy basil belong to the same family.

Picture on page 30   *Serves 4*

250 gms bright red tomatoes (without any yellow patches near the stem end)

½ cup chopped fresh sweet basil leaves or ¼ cup chopped tulsi leaves

1 medium onion

1 celery stalk - chopped (2- 3 tbsp)

1 tsp chopped garlic

1 tbsp olive oil or any cooking oil

1¼ tsp salt, ½ tsp black pepper, ½ tsp orgeano, ¼ tsp sugar

2½ cups readymade coconut milk

2 tbsp readymade tomato puree

finely chopped greens of 1 spring onion (hara pyaz)

1. Cut each tomato into 4 pieces and onion into 8 pieces.
2. Chop the celery stem as shown (only stem is used).
3. Place tomatoes, onion, chopped celery stem, garlic & oil in a pan. Cover & cook over low heat for 15-20 minutes, stirring in between. Remove from fire. Add ½ cup water, salt, pepper, orgeano and sugar. Cool. Keep aside.
4. Put cooled mixture in a mixer & churn till smooth.
5. Strain through a strainer (chhanni) pressing with the back of a spoon. Put the mixture in the same pan and keep on fire.
6. Add 2½ cups coconut milk, basil and tomato puree and bring to a boil. Reduce heat.
7. Add greens of spring onion. Remove from fire. Serve hot in indiviual soup bowls.

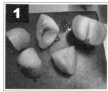

Note: In absence of sweet basil you can use half the amount of tender tulsi leaves or coriander leaves.

Cilantro (coriander) Soup

Serves 3-4

1 tsp butter, 1 bay leaf (tej patta), 1" stick cinnamon (dalchini)
¾ cup chopped potato, ½ cup milk
1 cup cilantro or green coriander chopped with the stalks
STOCK
2½ cups water, 1 veg seasoning cube (maggi or knorr)

1. For the stock, crush 1 seasoning cube and mix with 2½ cups of water. Keep aside.
2. Peel potato and cut into small cubes or pieces.
3. Melt 1 tsp butter in a pan, add bay leaf, cinnamon and chopped potato. Cook for 5 minutes on medium flame, stirring in between.
4. Add 1 cup chopped coriander, cook for 1 minute.
5. Reduce heat. Add ½ cup milk. Cook for 2 minutes on medium flame, stirring continuously. Remove from fire. Let it cool.
6. Churn cooled mixture in a mixer to get a puree.
7. Return puree to the pan, add the prepared stock. Give 2-3 boils. Remove from fire. Serve in individual soup bowls. Serve hot.

Gaspacho

A classic, cold Spanish soup.

Serves 4

4 large red tomatoes - chopped
2 flakes garlic - chopped, 1 medium cucumber - diced
2 slices bread - sides removed, soaked in water & squeezed
1 tbsp chopped parsley, 1 tbsp vinegar
1½ tsp sugar, 1¼ tsp salt, 2 tsp olive oil
½ tsp black pepper, a pinch of red chilli powder
1 tsp tabasco sauce, 1 tray ice cubes
1 tbsp each of - finely chopped onion, capsicum and cream, for garnish

1. Put the tomatoes in a pan with 1 cup water. Boil. Keep on low flame till they turn soft. Remove from fire. Cool.
2. Churn the cooled tomatoes, with garlic, cucumber, bread, parsley and vinegar in a blender to a puree.
3. Strain mixture. Add sugar, salt, olive oil, pepper and red chilli powder.
4. Add tabasco to taste. Add the ice cubes. The ice as it melts, gives enough liquid to make the soup thin. Garnish with finely diced onion and capsicum, and cream if desired.

Spring Onion & Potato Soup

Serves 4-5

BOIL TOGETHER
1 spring onion - chopped upto the greens
1 potato - chopped
8-10 peppercorns (saboot kali mirch)
½" piece ginger - chopped
1 tsp salt, or to taste
4 cups water

OTHER INGREDIENTS
1 cup milk
2 tsp lemon juice (juice of ½ lemon)
salt to taste
½ tsp butter

GARNISH
2-3 almonds (badam)- roasted on a griddle (tawa) and very thinly sliced

1. Boil spring onion, potato, peppercorns, ginger, salt and water together in a pan. After the boil keep on low heat and cook covered, for about 15 minutes, till potatoes turn soft.

2. Remove from fire. Strain and keep the liquid aside. Cool. Blend the onions etc. to a green puree with a little liquid.
3. Add the rest of the liquid and 1 cup milk to the green puree. Keep on fire. Boil. Simmer on low heat for 5-7 minutes.

4. Add salt to taste and ½ tsp of butter if desired. Remove from fire.
5. Add lemon juice, mix well. Serve hot garnished with some roasted and finely sliced almonds.

Burnt Corn Soup

Picture on facing page   *Serves 2-3*

1 big corn on the cob (bhutta), about 250-275 gms
1 green capsicum - washed
2 vegetable seasoning cubes (Maggi or Knorr), see page 14
½ tsp salt
2-3 tbsp butter or olive oil
½ onion - finely chopped
¼ tsp finely chopped garlic
1 tsp finely chopped coriander leaves
1 tsp lemon juice

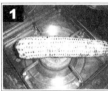

1. Roast whole corn on a naked flame, turning sides, constantly till brown specks appear on all the sides.
2. Remove from fire. Scrape roasted corn niblets with the help of a knife from the cob. Keep aside 2 tbsp corn for garnishing.

38

Contd...

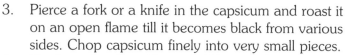

3. Pierce a fork or a knife in the capsicum and roast it on an open flame till it becomes black from various sides. Chop capsicum finely into very small pieces.

4. Crush stock cubes. Mix with 1½ cups of warm water and keep aside the stock.
5. Heat butter or oil in a saucepan or any deep pan. Add chopped onion and cook till onions turn soft. Cook for 3-4 minutes on medium flame.
6. Add garlic & roasted corn niblets. Cook for 2 minutes.

7. Add prepared stock, capsicum and salt. Give one boil.
8. Lower heat. Cook covered for 5 minutes. Remove from fire and cool. Blend coarsely in mixer to a rough paste.

9. Put this paste in the saucepan. Return to fire. Add 1½ cups of water, coriander and lemon juice. Mix well. Give one boil. Simmer for a minute.
10. Remove from fire. Serve garnished with corn niblets.

◅ *Sweet Corn Vegetable Soup : Recipe on page 46*

Recipe on page 46

41

Cheesy Mushroom Soup

Serves 8

200 gm mushrooms - chopped into very thin, small pieces
½ tbsp butter, 1 large onion - sliced thinly, ½" piece ginger - grated finely
2 cups of milk mixed with 3 tbsp cornflour
2 tsp salt, or to taste & white pepper to taste
2-3 tbsp chopped coriander, juice of ½ lemon
1 cube (20 gm) grated cheese - to garnish

1. Heat ½ tbsp butter in a pressure cooker. Add onion and ginger. Stir.
2. Add the mushrooms and stir for 2-3 minutes.
3. Add 6 cups of water and close the lid of the pressure cooker and pressure cook to give 1-2 whistles. Simmer on low heat for ½ minute. Remove from heat. Drop pressure by putting the cooker under water. Open the lid.
4. Return the pressure cooker to heat without the lid. Dissolve cornflour in milk and add to the soup. Add salt, white pepper and coriander. Boil. Simmer for 1 minute.
5. Remove from fire and mix in the lemon juice. Stir gently to mix. Serve hot garnished with grated cheese.

CHINESE & THAI Soups

Lemon Coriander Soup

Serves 4

CLEAR STOCK

6 cups water
1 stick lemon grass - chopped or rind of 1 lemon (1 tsp rind)
¼ cup chopped coriander alongwith stalks
1" piece of ginger - washed, sliced without peeling
2 laung (cloves), 1 tej patta (bay leaf)
2 seasoning cubes (maggi or knorr or any other brand)

OTHER INGREDIENTS

1 tbsp oil, ¼ tsp red chilli flakes
½ carrot- - cut into paper thin slices, 2 mushrooms - cut into paper thin slices
2 baby corns - cut into paper thin slices
1 tsp salt & ¼ tsp pepper to taste

Contd...

2 tbsp lemon juice, 1 tsp sugar, or to taste
2 tbsp coriander leaves - torn roughly with the hands
2 tbsp cornflour dissolved in ¼ cup water

1. If using lemon rind, wash and grate 1 lemon with the peel gently on the finest side of the grater to get lemon rind. Do not apply pressure and see that the white pith beneath the lemon peel is not grated along with the yellow rind. The white pith is bitter!

2. Cut mushrooms into thin slices.
3. Cut carrot into paper thin slices diagonally (¼ cup).
4. For stock, mix all ingredients given under clear stock with 6 cups of water. Bring to a boil. Keep on low flame for 5 minutes. Strain the stock. If there is lemon grass, pick up most of the pieces and put back in the stock. Keep aside.

5. Heat 1 tsp oil in a wok. Remove from fire. Add ¼ tsp red chilli flakes.
6. Immediately, add carrot, mushrooms and baby corns cut into paper thin slices. Return to fire. Add

pepper. Saute for 1 minute on medium flame.

7. Add the prepared stock into the vegetables in the wok. Boil. Add 1 tsp salt and sugar.

8. Add 2 tbsp cornflour dissolved in ¼ cup water, stirring continuously. Boil.

9. Add lemon juice and coriander leaves. Simmer for 1-2 minutes. Check salt, sugar and lemon juice. Add more if required. Remove from fire.

10. Add a few more green coriander leaves. Serve hot in soup bowls.

Sweet Corn Vegetable Soup

Picture on page 40   *Serves 6*

1 readymade cream style sweet corn tin (460 gm), about 2½ cups
¼ cup finely chopped carrot
¼ cup finely chopped cabbage
1 spring onion - finely chopped alongwith the greens
2-3 french beans - finely chopped, 2 tbsp green chilli sauce
1 tbsp red chill sauce
1 tbsp vinegar
¼ tsp pepper, 2 tsp level salt
a pinch of ajinomoto
5 tbsp cornflour dissolved in ¾ cup water

1. Mix cream style corn with 9 cups water in a deep pan. Bring to a boil. Boil for 5 minutes.
2. Add chilli sauces and vinegar. Simmer for 1-2 minutes.
3. Meanwhile heat 1 tbsp oil in a nonstick pan add

the vegetables. Saute for 1 minute. Add the sauteed vegetables to the simmering soup. Simmer for 1 minute.

4. Add salt, pepper and ajinomoto to the soup.
5. Add cornflour paste and cook for 2-3 minutes till the soup thickens. Serve hot.

Sweet Corn Soup with Fresh Corn

Grate 4 large corn-on-cobs (saboot bhutte), about 1 kg, keeping aside ¼ cup of whole corn kernels without grating them. Pressure cook grated and whole corn kernels with 10 cups water and 1½ tbsp sugar to give 2 whistles. Keep on low heat for 10 minutes. Continue from step 2.

Orient Noodle Soup

A spicy, hot, clear soup with lots of vegetables for the winter months. Lemon rind and tomato puree add a delicious flavour to this appetizer soup. Noodles make it different.

Picture on facing page   *Serves 4*

1½ tbsp oil
3 flakes garlic - chopped & crushed
4 mushrooms - sliced and then cut into thin long pieces
1 small carrot - grated, ½ capsicum - finely chopped
10-12 spinach leaves - shredded finely (cut into thin strips)
3 tbsp ready-made tomato puree
½ tsp red chilli flakes
30 gms noodles (½ cup) - break into 2" pieces
1¼ tsp salt, ¼ tsp pepper, 1 tsp sugar
rind of 1 lemon (1 tsp approx.)
2 tsp green chilli sauce
1 tsp vinegar
2 stock cubes - crushed

Contd...

1. To take out lemon rind, grate a firm whole lemon on the finest holes of the grater without applying too much pressure. Grate only the upper yellow skin without grating the white bitter pith beneath the yellow skin. Keep rind aside.
2. Heat oil in a pan. Reduce heat and add garlic and red chilli flakes. Saute briefly for ½ minute.
3. Add mushrooms, carrot and capsicum. Stir fry for 1 minute.
4. Add tomato puree & red chillies. Stir for ½ minute.
5. Add 4 cups of water. Crush 2 stock cubes in it. Bring the soup to a boil. Add the noodles. Boil on medium heat for 2-3 minutes till noodles are soft.
6. Add salt, pepper, sugar, lemon rind, chilli sauce and vinegar.
7. Add the finely shredded spinach, simmer for 1 minute. Serve hot in soup bowls.

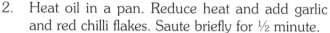

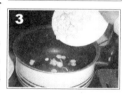

◁ *Tomato Rasam : Recipe on page 70*

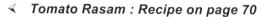

Hot & Sour

The popular Chinese soup. An all time favourite!

Picture on cover   *Serves 4-5*

CHILLI-GARLIC PASTE
3 dry red chillies - deseeded and soaked in water for 10 minutes
2 flakes garlic, 1 tsp vinegar, 2 tbsp water

OTHER INGREDIENTS
2 tbsp oil, 1-2 tender french beans - sliced very finely (3-4 tbsp)
1-2 tbsp dried mushrooms or 2-3 fresh mushrooms - chopped
½ cup chopped cabbage
½ cup thickly grated carrot
2 vegetable seasoning cubes (maggi) - powdered, orcrushed
1 tbsp tomato ketchup
1 tsp sugar, 1¼ tsp salt, ½ tsp pepper powder, or to taste
2 tbsp soya sauce, 1½ tbsp vinegar
6 tbsp cornflour mixed with ½ cup water

1. Soak dry, red chillies in a little water for 10 minutes.
2. For the chilli-garlic paste, drain the red chillies. Grind red chillies, garlic and vinegar roughly with 2 tbsp water in a small coffee or spice grinder.
3. If dried mushrooms are available, soak them in hot water for ½ hour to soften. Wash thoroughly to clean the dirt in them. Cut away the hard stem portion and then cut into smaller pieces.
4. Heat 2 tbsp oil. Add beans and mushrooms. Stir fry for 1-2 minutes on high flame. Add cabbage and carrots. Stir for a few seconds.
5. Add chilli-garlic paste, sugar, salt, pepper, soya sauce, vinegar and tomato ketchup. Boil for 2 minutes.
6. Add 6 cups of water and the seasoning cubes.
7. Add cornflour paste, stirring continuously. Cook for 2-3 minutes till the soup turns thick. Check salt and remove from fire. Serve hot.

Tom Yum

A clear lemon flavoured Thai soup with paper thin slices of vegetables.

Picture on page 30   *Serves 4*

3- 4 mushrooms - cut into paper thin slices
1 small carrot - cut into paper thin diagonal slices
2 fresh red chillies - sliced diagonally and deseeded
3-4 kaffir lime leaves (nimbu ke patte)
2 tbsp chopped coriander leaves
1" piece ginger - chopped finely or cut into paper thin slices
1 stalk lemon grass - cut into thin slices diagonally, see next page
juice of 1 lemon

PASTE
2 dry red chillies
2-3 flakes garlic
2 tbsp oil
½ onion - chopped
½ tsp salt

1. Cut mushrooms and carrots into paper thin slices.
2. Prepare a paste by grinding all the ingredients of the paste in a mixer.
3. In a deep pan put 5 cups water, sliced ginger, lime or lemon leaves and lemon grass. Add the above red chilli paste also to the water. After the boil, keep covered on low heat for 5 minutes.
4. Add mushrooms, carrots, red chillies and coriander. Boil for 2 minutes on medium flame.
5. Reduce heat. Add lemon juice and salt to taste. Simmer for 1 minute. Pour into individual bowls and serve hot.

About Lemon Grass

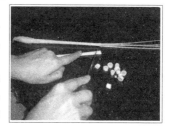

Only the light green stem of lemon grass is edible. The upper grass like portion has a lot of flavour but is not edible. So to use lemon grass, remove the grass portion. Discard 1" hard portion from the base of the stalk of lemon grass and then cut the stalk into thin slices. Tie the remaining grass portion into a knot. You can put this flavourful knot in soups and discard it at serving time.

Manchow Soup

Serves 6

3 tbsp oil
4 flakes garlic - crushed (½ tsp)
1 tsp very finely chopped ginger
1 cup finely chopped mushrooms (6-8 mushrooms)
1 cup finely shredded (cut into thin 1" long pieces) cabbage
1½ small carrots - thinly cut into round slices or flowers, (1 cup)
½ tsp pepper, or to taste
a pinch of ajinomoto
3-4 drops of soya sauce
2 tsp chilli sauce, 1 tsp vinegar
2 vegetable seasoning cubes (maggi, knorr or any other)
6 cups water
salt to taste
6 tbsp cornflour dissolved in 1 cup water

GARNISH (OPTIONAL)
½ cup noodles - deep fried till crisp

1. Heat 3 tbsp oil. Reduce heat. Add garlic and ginger. Stir on low heat.
2. Add mushrooms. Stir for a minute on medium flame.
3. Add cabbage and carrot. Stir for a minute.
4. Reduce heat. Add pepper, ajinomoto, a few drops soya sauce, chilli sauce and vinegar. Stir to mix well.

5. Add 6 cups water and bring to a boil. Crush 2 seasoning cube and add to the boiling water. Mix. Simmer for 2-3 minutes. Check salt and add more according to taste.
6. Add dissolved cornflour. Bring to a boil, stirring constantly. Simmer for 2 minutes.

7. Serve in soup bowls, garnished with some crisp fried noodles.

Wonton Vegetable Soup

Serves 6

WONTON WRAPPERS
1 cup plain flour (maida)
½ tsp salt
1 tbsp oil
a little water (chilled)

WONTON FILLING
½ of a small onion - finely chopped
½ carrot - chopped very finely
8 french beans - chopped very finely or
1 cup chopped mushrooms
½ cup cabbage - finely chopped
a pinch of ajinomoto (optional)
½ tsp white pepper, salt to taste
½ tsp sugar
1 tsp soya sauce

WONTON SOUP
6 cups vegetable stock, see page 13 or 14
2 spring onions - chopped finely alongwith the greens
1 tbsp soya sauce
1 tsp white pepper
1 tsp sugar
¼ tsp ajinomoto (optional)

1. To prepare the wonton wrappers, sift plain flour and salt.
2. Add oil and rub with finger tips till the flour resembles bread crumbs. Add chilled water gradually and make a stiff dough. Knead the dough well for about 4-5 minutes till smooth. Cover dough with a damp cloth. Keep aside for ½ hour.
3. To prepare the filling, heat 1 tbsp oil. Stir fry onions, for a few seconds.
4. Add all other vegetables. Stir fry for 1-2 minutes. Add ajinomoto, pepper, salt, sugar and soya sauce. Mix. Remove from fire. Cool filling before making wontons.
5. Divide the dough into 4 balls. Roll out each ball into thin chappatis.

Contd...

6. Cut into 2" squares. (a) Place some filling in centre. (b) Fold in half by lifting one corner & joining to the opposite corner to make a triangle. Press sides together. (c) Fold a little again, pressing firmly at both sides of the filling, but leaving corners open.

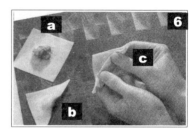

7. Bring 2 corners together, and cross over infront of the filling. Brush lightly with water where they meet, to make them stick. Keep wontons aside. (The wontons may be folded into different shapes like money bags, nurses caps or envelopes).

8. To serve the soup, boil vegetable stock, add the prepared wontons. Cover and cook for 12-15 minutes on low flame till they float on the top.

9. Add spring onions, soya sauce, pepper, sugar and ajinomoto. Simmer for 1- 2 minutes. Remove from fire. Serve hot.

Talomein Soup

Serves 4

4 cups vegetable stock (see page 13 or 14)
½ carrot - peeled
3-4 cabbage leaves - roughly torn, 1 cup boiled noodles
1 tsp salt, or to taste, ½ tsp each of sugar, black pepper
1 tsp soya sauce, a pinch ajinomoto (optional)
2 tbsp cornflour dissolved in ½ cup water

1. Boil 5 cups of water in a large pan. Add 2 tsp salt and 1 tsp sugar to the water. Add peeled carrot to the boiling water. Boil. Keep on boiling for 1-2 minutes. Drain. Refresh in cold water. Cut into thin leaves or diagonal slices. Keep aside.
2. Mix stock, salt, sugar, pepper, soya sauce & ajinomoto in a pan. Boil.
3. Add cornflour paste, stirring continuously.
4. Add carrots and cabbage. Boil for 2-3 minutes.
5. Add boiled noodles, remove from fire. Serve.

Mushroom Crispy Rice Soup

Serves 6

½ cup boiled rice - spread on a tray for 10 minutes and
deep fried till golden
1 cup sliced fresh mushrooms, 1 onion - sliced
1 tbsp crushed ginger, 6 cups water
1 tbsp soya sauce, 1 tbsp vinegar, 1 tsp sugar
1 tsp white pepper, salt to taste
2 tbsp cornflour dissolved in ¼ cup water, 2 tbsp oil

1. Prepare vegetable stock as given on page 13 or 14.
2. Slice mushrooms finely.
3. Heat oil. Add sliced onion and stir till soft. Add mushrooms. Stir fry for 2 minutes.
4. Add crushed ginger. Stir fry for ½ minute.
5. Add water.
6. Add all the other ingredients except cornflour paste. Boil.
7. Add cornflour paste. Cook for 1 minute till the soup turns thick.
8. Serve soup garnished with deep fried rice.

Stir fried Vegetable Soup

Serves 4

½ cup grated carrot, 1 cup grated cabbage
1 tsp oil, 1 tsp soya sauce, 2 tsp chilli sauce
½ tsp salt, ½ tsp pepper, or to taste
4 cups vegetable stock (see page 13 or 14) or water
3 tbsp cornflour - dissolved in ½ cup water
¼-½ cup paneer - finely diced
2 tbsp lemon juice

1. Heat 1 tsp oil. Add carrot and cabbage. Stir for a minute.
2. Add soya sauce, chilli sauce, salt and pepper. Add 4 cups vegetable stock or water. Give 2-3 boils.

3. Dissolve cornflour in ½ cup water, stir well. Add the cornflour paste into the soup. Stir till it boils. Remove when thick. Add some more cornflour dissolved in water, if the soup appears thin.
4. Add tiny cubes of paneer. Add lemon juice and serve hot.

INDIAN SOUPS
&
SHORBAS

Everyday Vegetable Soup

Serves 4

2 carrots - chopped (1 cup), 1 onion - chopped roughly
1 large potato - roughly chopped or 1 large turnip (shalgam) - roughly
chopped or 1 cup chopped lauki (bottle gourd)
½ cup cabbage - roughly chopped, 2 tomatoes - chopped (1 cup)
2 bay leaves (tej pata), 2 laung (cloves)
¾ cup milk, 1 tsp salt and ½ pepper or to taste

1. Place carrots, onion, potato or turnip or lauki, cabbage, tomatoes, bay leaves and laung in a pressure cooker with 4 cups water. Pressure cook to give 2 whistles. Simmer on low heat for 5 minutes. Remove from fire.

2. Cool and puree the soup in a mixer or a food processor. Strain the soup.

3. Put the pureed soup back on fire. Add ¾ cup milk to the soup. Stir continuously till it boils. Reduce heat.

4. Add salt and pepper. Cook for 2-3 minutes on low heat. Serve hot.

Note: You can add 1 tsp butter to the soup at step 4 for a richer taste.

Hari Moong ka Shorba

A very light delicious soup which makes a good start to an Indian meal.

Serves 4-6

1 cup green saboot moong dal - soak for ½ hour in some water
1½ tbsp jaggery powder (gur)
¼ tsp haldi, 1½ tsp salt, 2 tbsp lemon juice
3-4 tbsp coriander - chopped

COLLECT TOGETHER
¼ tsp hing (asafoetida)
½ tsp jeera (cumin seeds)
½ tsp rai (mustard seeds), 3-4 laung (cloves)
1" stick dalchini (cinnamon)
3-4 saboot kali mirch (peppercorns)
8-10 curry leaves

GRIND TO A PASTE (1½ TSP)
½" piece ginger, ½ green chilli , 3-4 flakes garlic

1. Soak dal for ½ hour. Drain water from the soaked dal. Add 10 cups water and salt. Cook covered for about ½ hour till the dal is done. Do not pressure cook.
2. Heat 2 tbsp oil in a heavy bottom deep pan. Add all the collected ingredients together - hing, jeera, rai, dalchini, laung, peppercorns and curry patta. Stir.
3. Add 1½ tsp of the prepared ginger-garlic-green chilli paste. Stir.
4. Strain the water of the dal into the pan. Do not mash the dal at all.
5. Add jaggery, haldi and salt to taste. Simmer for 2 minutes.
6. Add lemon juice and coriander. Serve hot.

Microwaved Cauliflower Soup

Picture on page 1   *Serves 4*

2 cups small cauliflower florets
2 tbsp butter or oil
½ red bell pepper (capsicum) - cut into thin strips
1 large onion - finely chopped
a pinch of chilli powder or to taste
2 cups water, 1 veg seasoning cube (maggi or knorr)
a pinch of haldi, 1 cup milk
2 tbsp besan
2 tbsp chopped fresh coriander

1. Cut cauliflower into small florets.
2. Put butter or oil in a large microwave-safe dish and microwave for 30 seconds.
3. Add the cauliflower, capsicum and onion. Mix. Cook on high for 8-10 minutes.

4. Add chilli powder, haldi, seasoning cube and water. Mix well. Cover and cook on high for 4 minutes.

5. Meanwhile, add a little of the milk to the besan to make a paste. Gradually stir in the remaining milk, then stir the besan mixture and coriander into the soup. Mix. Cover and cook on high for 6 minutes. Serve hot.

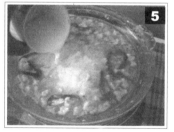

Tomato Rasam

A light and spicy South Indian appetizer. Best enjoyed with papad!

Picture on page 50   *Serves 4*

5-6 tomatoes - whole
salt to taste (1½ tsp approx.), ¼ tsp haldi (turmeric) powder
¼ tsp hing (asafoetida) powder
coriander leaves for garnishing

RASAM POWDER
5 dry whole red chillies
3 tsp saboot dhania (coriander seeds)
¼ tsp sarson (mustard seeds)
½ tsp jeera (cumin seeds)
8-10 curry leaves, 1 tsp oil

1. Boil whole tomatoes with 1 cup of water. Keep on low flame for 10 minutes till tomatoes turn soft. Remove from fire and add another 2 cups of water. Cool and churn in a mixer to get a smooth puree.

2. Strain the pureed tomatoes through a strainer to extract juice. Discard skins and keep tomato juice aside.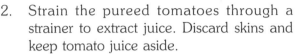

3. Prepare the rasam powder by frying all the ingredients of the powder together on a tawa or in a kadhai on very low flame for 3-4 minutes, till it turns fragrant and starts to smell. Powder finely.

4. To the tomato juice, add salt and haldi. Boil.

5. Add 2 tsp of rasam powder 1 cup water and hing powder. Simmer for 10 minutes. Remove from fire. Serve in glasses garnished with coriander leaves and serve hot with papads.

Subziyon Ka Shorba

Mixed vegetables in a tomato based shorba, tempered with cumin.

Serves 4

500 gm tomatoes - chopped roughly
1 potato - peeled and chopped roughly
3-4 flakes garlic - crushed or chopped
1" piece ginger - chopped
1 green chilli - chopped
10-12 leaves of poodina (mint)
¼ tsp red chilli powder
1 tsp salt & ½ tsp sugar, or to taste

TEMPERING (CHOWK)
1 tbsp butter or oil, 1 tsp jeera (cumin seeds)
mixed vegetables - 1 small floret cauliflower, ½ carrot
1" piece of cabbage & 1-2 French beans

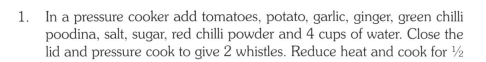

1. In a pressure cooker add tomatoes, potato, garlic, ginger, green chilli poodina, salt, sugar, red chilli powder and 4 cups of water. Close the lid and pressure cook to give 2 whistles. Reduce heat and cook for ½ minute.

2. Meanwhile chop the beans into very tiny pieces and grate the cabbage, cauliflower and carrot coarsely. If you wish cut all the vegetables very finely instead of grating them. The mixed vegetables should be about 1 cup.

3. Remove the pressure cooker from heat. Drop the pressure by putting the cooker under water.

4. Open the lid and strain the soup through a soup strainer, pressing with a metal spoon or ladle (karchhi) to get all the extract. Discard the residue. Keep the shorba aside.

5. Heat butter or oil in a clean pan. Add jeera. Wait till it turns golden. Add the vegetables and stir fry for 1 minute.

6. Add the strained shorba and bring to a boil. Cook covered till the vegetables turn slightly tender. Adjust the seasonings.

7. Garnish with chopped mint and serve hot in soup bowls with a spoon.

Tomato & Coriander Shorba

Serves 6

1 kg (12 medium) red tomatoes - chopped roughly
4 tsp besan (gram flour), 1 tbsp oil, 1 tsp jeera (cumin seeds)
8-10 curry leaves, 2-3 green chillies - slit lengthwise
1 tsp sugar or to taste
½ cup finely chopped fresh coriander, 1 tsp salt or to taste
1 tsp lemon juice or to taste

1. Pressure cook the tomatoes with 2 cups water to give one whistle. Keep on low flame for 5-7 minutes. Remove from fire.
2. When it cools down, blend in a mixer. Strain & keep tomato juice aside.
3. Add besan to 4 cups water and blend well in the mixer. Keep aside.
4. Heat oil in a pan and reduce flame. Add jeera. Let it turn golden.
5. Add curry leaves, green chillies, tomato juice, water mixed with besan and sugar. Boil.
6. Add coriander leaves and salt to taste.
7. Cook for 4-5 minutes. Add lemon juice to taste. Serve hot.

2 Layer Tomato-Broccoli Soup : Recipe on page 78 ➤

HEAVY SOUPS FOR A COMPLETE MEAL

◁ *Minestrone : Recipe on page 80*

2 Layer Tomato-Broccoli Soup

A delicious tomato soup topped with a healthy broccoli topping.

Picture on page 75   *Serves 6*

1 small onion - chopped roughly
1 carrot - chopped roughly, 1 small potato - chopped roughly
½ kg (5-6) ripe red tomatoes - chopped roughly, 1 tsp butter
1" stick dalchini (cinnamon)
4-5 saboot kali mirch (peppercorns), 3-4 laung (cloves)
1 tsp tomato ketchup, 4 tbsp thick cream
1½ tsp salt and ½ tsp pepper or to taste

2ND LAYER (TOPPING)
½ cup chopped broccoli, ¼ tsp salt, ¼ tsp pepper

1. Melt 1 tbsp butter in a pressure cooker, add dalchini, saboot kali mirch and laung. Stir for 30 seconds.
2. Add chopped onion, carrot and potato. Stir for about 3-4 minutes, till onion starts to change colour.

3. Add the chopped tomatoes and cook for 2-3 minutes.
4. Add 3 cups of water and 1 tsp salt. Cover the pressure cooker and pressure cook to give 1-2 whistles. Simmer for 3-4 minutes. Remove from heat and cool. Strain and reserve the liquid as well as the solids in the strainer.
5. Blend the solids to a smooth puree. Mix the strained liquid with the puree to get a soup.
6. Reheat the soup in a saucepan. Check salt, pepper. Add more if required. Keep aside.
7. In a separate pan heat 2 tsp butter, add chopped broccoli, saute for 2 minutes. Add ¼ tsp salt, pepper and ¾ cup water. Give one boil. Remove from fire. Cool and churn in a mixer to a smooth thick puree. Add 1 tbsp water. Keep aside.
8. To serve, separately reheat the tomato soup and the broccoli topping to a boil. Pour the prepared tomato soup in serving bowls. Swirl 2 tbsp of hot broccoli topping over the tomato soup in each bowl. Serve immediately.

Minestrone

Picture on page 76   *Serves 4-5*

2 tbsp olive oil or any cooking oil
1 onion - chopped finely (½ cup)
2 flakes garlic - crushed
1 small potato - diced into very small pieces (½ cup)
1 carrot - diced into small pieces (½ cup)
3-4 tbsp finely chopped celery or green french beans
3 medium sized tomatoes - blanched, peeled and chopped finely
2-3 tbsp baked beans, (optional) see note
¼ cup of macaroni or any other small pasta
5 cups stock or 5 cups water mixed with 2 seasoning cubes, see note
salt & pepper to taste

1. To blanch the tomatoes, put them in boiling water for 3-4 minutes. Remove from water and peel them to remove skin. Chop them finely. Keep aside.

2. Heat oil. Add onion & garlic. Stir fry till light brown.
3. Add carrots and potatoes & stir fry for 1-2 minutes.
4. Add diced macaroni. Stir for 1-2 minutes.
5. Add celery and tomatoes. Cook 2-3 minutes.
6. Add stock and baked beans.
7. Give one boil. Lower heat. Cover and simmer for 15 minutes. Add salt and pepper to taste and mix well.
8. Serve hot, garnished with some grated cheese (optional).

Note:

- Instead of stock (made at home), 5 cups water and 2 seasoning cubes can be used. Mix both together and use as required. Do not add any salt, if using soup cubes as they already contain salt. Taste at the end and adjust salt to taste.
- The left over baked beans can be stored in a clean stainless steel or a plastic container in the freezer compartment of the refrigerator without getting spoilt for a month.

Pasta & Bean Soup

Serves 4

1 cup (kidney beans) rajmah, (use ½ cup red and ½ cup chitra (white)
rajmah) - soaked together in water overnight or for 6-8 hours
1 tbsp oil
2 spring onions - thinly sliced including the greens
1-2 garlic flakes - crushed
1 cup sliced baby corns
2 vegetable seasoning cubes - crushed
5 tbsp tiny soup pasta
3 tbsp tomato puree
4 tbsp finely chopped red capsicum or deseeded chopped tomatoes
2-3 drops of tabasco sauce, or to taste
salt and black pepper to taste

1. Drain the soaked beans and place in a pressure cooker with 5 cups
water. After the first whistle, reduce heat and keep on low flame for 15
minutes. Do not make them too soft. Cook until nearly tender.

2. Heat the oil in a large pan and fry white part of spring onion, garlic and baby corns for 2 minutes.

3. Add the seasoning cubes and the beans with about 4 cups of their liquid.

4. Add the pasta. Cover and simmer for 10 minutes or till the pasta gets cooked.

5. Stir in the tomato puree, spring onion greens and red capsicum or tomato pieces.

6. Add tabasco sauce, salt and pepper. Remove from fire. Serve hot.

Useful Tip

I always keep boiled rajmahs stored in a box in the freezer compartment of my refrigerator. They come in very handy to make soups or just for topping a piece of garlic toast with some cheese sprinkled on it. I even use them in my baked dishes.

Slicing of Green Onions

Deseeding the Tomatoes

Mulligatawny

A lentil soup, pepped up with black pepper! Also called "pepper water".

Picture on page 103   Serves 4-5

¼ cup dhuli masoor dal (orange dal) - soaked for atleast 1 hour, or more
1½ tbsp butter
2 onions - chopped
2 carrots - chopped
1 small apple - peeled and chopped
1½ tbsp curry powder (MDH)
2 vegetable seasoning cubes (maggi) mixed with 5 cups water
1½ tsp salt
¾ tsp freshly crushed peppercorns (saboot kali mirch)
¼ cup boiled rice
1½ tbsp lemon juice, or to taste

GARNISH
1-2 tbsp finely chopped coriander

1. Strain water from the dal. Keep aside.
2. Heat butter in a deep pan. Add onion, carrots and apple. Stir for 3-4 minutes till onions turn very light brown.
3. Add curry powder and stir for ½ minute only.
4. Add dal. Add water mixed with seasoning cubes. Boil. Cover and simmer for 20 minutes or till dal turns soft.
5. Remove from fire. Let it cool. After it cools, grind to a puree. Strain the soup through a soup sieve.
6. Put soup back on fire. Add salt and pepper. Add rice. Check salt. Cook for 2 minutes.
7. Add lemon juice and remove from fire. Serve hot in soup bowls, garnished with some chopped coriander.

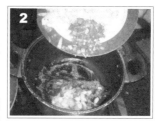

Spiced Pumpkin Soup

Serves 6

2 tbsp butter
1 onion - finely chopped
3 cups deseeded, peeled and cubed pumpkin (kaddu, sitaphal) choose
unripe one with greenish skin and whitish from inside
1 tbsp flour (maida)
a pinch of grated jaiphal (nutmeg)
½ tsp dalchini powder (ground cinnamon)
2½ cups water mixed with 1 vegetable seasoning cube to make stock
1 cup ready made orange juice
¼ tsp brown sugar (optional)
¼ tsp salt, ½ tsp oregano, ½ tsp black pepper
1 tsp butter, 1½ tbsp lemon juice

TOPPING
1 tbsp magaz (melon seeds) or almonds cut into thin long pieces
1 bread slice - to make a few croutons, see page 11

1. Heat 2 tbsp butter in a large deep pan, add the onion and pumpkin. Stir fry for 4-5 minutes.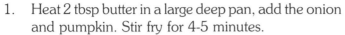
2. Add maida, jaiphal and dalchini powder. Cook covered for 2 minutes, stirring occasionally.
3. Add 1 cup stock, orange juice, brown sugar and salt. Reduce heat and simmer for 10 minutes, until the pumpkin has softened. Remove from fire. Cool.
4. Churn pumpkin mixture until smooth. Strain the soup. Return the pureed soup to the same pan.
5. Add the remaining stock, ½ cup water, oregano, pepper, 1 tsp butter, and lemon juice. Give one boil. Check salt and pepper. Keep aside.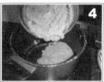
6. Toast melon seeds or almonds on a tawa for 1-2 minutes, till golden and fragrant. Serve the soup hot, topped with a few croutons (see page 11) and melon seeds or toasted almonds. Serve the remaining croutons separately.

Cheese Soup

Serves 5-6

2 tbsp oil or butter, 2 onions - chopped
3 medium potatoes - peeled & chopped
5 cups water, 1 cup milk
½ cup fresh cream mixed with 1 tsp lemon juice, 2 tbsp cheese spread
1 tsp salt, ½ tsp black pepper or to taste

GARNISHING
2 toasted slices of bread
2 cubes (40 gm) cheese, fresh coriander leaves
½ tsp peppercorns (saboot kali mirch) - crushed roughly

1. Put butter or oil in a pressure cooker. Add onions and stir till light brown.
2. Add potatoes and saute for 1-2 minutes. Add 5 cups water and give 3-4 whistles to the cooker. Remove from fire.
3. When cool, strain, keeping the liquid (stock) aside. Grind the pressure cooked onion and potatoes in the strainer. Put them in a mixer/grinder and grind to a puree with about 1 cup liquid (stock) kept aside.

4. Strain the puree through a strainer. Mix with the leftover stock.

5. Boil 1 cup milk separately in a clean pan. Remove from fire.

6. Boil the soup separately. Keeping the soup on very low flame (the soup should not be boiling) add the boiled milk and cheese spread, stirring continuously. Simmer for 2-3 minutes on low flame.

7. Add cream mixed with lemon juice, keeping the flame on very low heat and gently stirring continuously.

8. Immediately remove the soup from fire. Keep aside till serving time.

9. To serve, grate cheese on a toasted slice of bread and put it in a hot oven for 8-10 minutes till crisp from the bottom. Cut diagonally to form small triangles. Arrange a coriander leaf on each piece.

10. Heat the soup till it just starts to boil. Pour in bowls and put 1-2 pieces of cheese triangles in each serving. Serve sprinkled with freshly crushed pepper.

Macaroni & Corn Soup

Serves 4

1 tbsp butter, 1 onion - finely chopped, 4 flakes garlic - crushed
1¼ cups cream style corn (tinned)
3-4 tbsp chopped basil or coriander leaves
¼ cup uncooked macaroni (small sized)
2½ tsp salt, ½ tsp pepper, or to taste
3-4 drops of lemon juice
2-3 tbsp grated cheese, to garnish (use tin or cubes)

1. Heat oil. Stir fry onion and garlic on low heat till onion turns soft.
2. Add the creamed corn. Stir fry for a minute.
3. Add 5 cups water, basil or coriander and macaroni. Cook on medium heat, for about 8-10 minutes, till the macaroni is done.
4. Add salt and pepper to taste. Add lemon juice to taste.
5. Serve in soup bowls, garnished with some grated cheese.

Note: Transfer the left over tinned corn in a stainless steel box or a zip lock bag & store in the freezer compartment of the refrigerator for a month.

Green Chick Pea Soup

Serves 8

**½ cup kabuli channe (chick peas) - boiled (1 cup), 7 cups water
½ bunch spinach (palak) - finely chopped (4 cups)
2 tbsp finely chopped fresh coriander - finely chopped, ½ tsp sugar
2 tbsp lemon juice, 1½ tsp salt
pepper to taste, 2 tbsp curd for topping**

1. Soak ½ cup channas overnight in some water. Drain. Heat water in a pressure cooker and add channas and give 2 whistles.
2. Boil spinach and coriander with ½ cup water and ½ tsp sugar to retain colour. Keep uncovered on low flame for 3-4 minutes. Remove from fire. Let it cool. Grind the cooled spinach along with boiled channas to a smooth puree. Add water to the puree in the mixer.
3. Strain puree. Add salt, pepper and lemon juice to taste. Give one boil.
4. Serve hot mixed with a teaspoon of beaten curd.

Spinach & Mushroom Soup

Picture on facing page   *Serves 3-4*

1 cup roughly chopped spinach
6 mushrooms - sliced very finely (paper thin slices)
2 cups milk, ½ tbsp butter, 1 flake garlic - crushed
2 cups water mixed with 2 tbsp cornflour
4-6 peppercorns - crushed, 1 tsp salt, or to taste, 1 tsp lemon juice

1. Boil chopped spinach with milk. Cook uncovered, for about 5 minutes or till spinach softens. Remove from fire. Cool. Strain the spinach and reserve the milk.
2. Put spinach in a blender with a little milk and roughly blend. Do not blend too much. Keep spinach puree aside.
3. Heat ½ tbsp butter. Add garlic and stir. Add mushrooms and saute for 3-4 minutes. Add the spinach puree and the milk kept aside.
4. Add 2 cups water mixed with 2 tbsp cornflour. Stir till it boils. Cook stirring frequently for 3-4 minutes. Add salt and freshly crushed pepper.
5. Add lemon juice to taste. Remove from fire. Serve hot.

Tangy Carrot Soup

Serves 4

2 big (250 gms) carrots - peeled and chopped
1 potato - peeled and chopped, 1 tsp oil
1 onion - chopped, 8-10 peppercorns (saboot kali mirch)
1" piece ginger - chopped
4 cups vegetable stock or water
juice of one orange or ½ cup ready-made orange juice
2 tbsp chopped coriander
¾ tsp salt or to taste & pepper

1. Saute onion, peppercorns and ginger in 1 tsp oil in a non stick pan till onions start to change colour.
2. To it add carrots and potato. Stir for 2-3 minutes on low flame. Add water. Bring to a boil. Simmer on low flame for 10-15 minutes till the vegetables get cooked. Remove from fire.
3. Cool and grind to a puree in a blender. Strain the vegetable puree.
4. Add orange juice, coriander, salt and pepper. Boil. Serve hot or cold.

◄ *Kali Mirch Jeera Rasam : Recipe on page 98*

Dal & Tomato Rasam

Serves 4

2 tbsp arhar dal (pigeon peas)
4 large tomatoes - chopped roughly
1½ tsp salt, or to taste

TADKA, BAGHAR (TEMPERING)
a pinch of hing (asafoetida)
½ tsp jeera (cumin)
½ tsp rai (brown mustard), a few curry patta

RASAM POWDER
Dry roast these ingredients.
Cool and grind to make rasam powder. Store the excess.

1 tsp jeera (cumin seeds)
1 tsp saboot dhania (coriander seeds), 3-4 dry red chillies
½ tsp saboot kali mirch (peppercorns)
2 tsp channa dal (split Bengal gram)

1. Wash and cut tomatoes roughly.
2. Wash dal. Add arhar dal, tomatoes and salt. Add 4½ cups water and boil for 15-20 minutes on low medium flame till dal is done.
3. Remove from fire and strain. Mash the tomatoes well while straining.
4. To the liquid, add 2-3 tsp of rasam powder and give 2-3 boils. Keep aside.
5. For tadka, heat a kadhai. Add hing, after a few seconds add jeera, mustard and curry patta. Dry roast on low heat for 1-2 minutes.
6. When starts to change colour, add the mixture to the rasam. Serve hot in small glasses.

Tip: Try topping the rasam with 1 tsp desi ghee, for those who do not mind a little fat!

Kali Mirch Jeera Rasam

A hot, spicy rasam, delicious as an appetizer.

Picture on page 94   *Serves 4*

4 large tomatoes - chopped roughly
3 cups water
1 tsp jeera (cumin seeds) - powdered roughly
1 tsp saboot kali mirch (peppercorns) - powdered roughly
1 tsp sarson (mustard seeds)
1 tsp oil, a few curry leaves
8-10 flakes of garlic - chopped & crushed
¼ tsp haldi (turmeric powder)
1¼ tsp salt, or to taste

1. Boil the tomatoes with 1 cup water in a pan. Simmer for 10 minutes on low flame till tomatoes turn very soft.
2. Remove from fire and mash lightly. Add the remaining 2 cups water & mash a little. Strain the juice through a big strainer into another clean pan. Discard the peels.

3. Powder the jeera & kali mirch coarsely on a chakla belan. Keep aside.
4. Heat a heavy bottomed pan. Add mustard seeds. Dry roast mustard seeds on low heat for 1-2 minutes.

5. When it splutters, add 1 tsp oil, curry leaves and garlic. Stir a little, till garlic changes colour.
6. Add the coarsely powdered jeera and saboot kali mirch. Stir for ½ minute.
7. Add tomato juice and 1 cup water to it. Add haldi powder & salt. Boil. Simmer on low flame for 7-8 minutes. Check salt and remove from fire. Serve hot.

Tip: Try topping the rasam with 1 tsp desi ghee, for those who do not mind a little fat!

Tomato Vegetable Soup

Serves 6

6 tomatoes - roughly chopped, 1 onion - roughly chopped
1 big potato - roughly chopped, 2 moti illaichi (black cardamoms)
½" stick dalchini (cinnamon), 2 tsp salt or to taste
¼ cup shelled peas (matar), ½ cup very finely grated carrots (gajar)
½ cup shredded cabbage
¼ cup finely diced fresh paneer - cut into very thin and small pieces
1 tsp lemon juice or according to taste (optional)
3/4 tsp freshly ground pepper, a pinch of red chilli powder

1. Pressure cook roughly chopped tomatoes, onion and potato, 1 moti illaichi, dalchini, salt and 2 cups water in a pressure cooker. Give 3 whistles. Remove from fire.
2. After the pressure drops, cool and blend to a smooth puree in a mixer.
3. Strain the puree and add 2½ cups of water to the puree.
4. Add the peas, carrots & cabbage to the puree and boil till the peas are tender. Add paneer cubes, freshly ground pepper and red chilli powder.

Note: Add lemon juice to the soup if you like it a bit sour. Pepper can also be adjusted to taste.

Lauki and Tomato Soup

Serves 4

½ kg tomatoes - roughly chopped
250 gms (1 small) lauki or ghiya (bottle gourd) - peeled and chopped
½" piece ginger, 6-8 saboot kali mirch (peppercorns)
1 onion - chopped
1½ tsp salt, ½ tsp pepper or to taste
a pinch of sugar, fresh coriander to garnish

1. In a pressure cooker, boil the tomatoes, ghiya, ginger, saboot kali mirch and onion with 4 cups of water to give 1 whistle. Keep on low flame for 4-5 minutes. Remove from fire.
2. Cool and puree in a blender. Strain the puree. Boil soup. Add the salt, pepper and sugar. Add fresh coriander.
3. Simmer for a few minutes. Serve hot.

Note: For variation, instead of ghiya one may use 2 tbsp of moong dhuli dal and juice of half a lemon.

Try topping the soup with 1 tsp of butter, for those who do not mind a little fat!

Herbed Green Pea Soup

Delicious soup without a drop of oil!

Picture on back cover   *Serves 4*

1 cup shelled peas (matar)
½ cup chopped potatoes, 1 seasoning cube (maggi or knorr)
1 onion - chopped, 1" piece of ginger - grated
1" stick dalchini (cinnamon), 1 tsp jeera (cumin seeds)
1 cup chopped spinach (palak), 1 tbsp mint leaves (poodina)
1 tbsp coriander (hara dhania)
¼ tsp salt, ½ tsp pepper, or to taste, 1 vegetable stock cube

1. Boil peas, potatoes, onion, ginger, dalchini, jeera and 5 cups of water in a pan. Cook for 8-10 minutes.
2. When they are almost cooked, add spinach, mint, coriander and 1 cup water. Cook uncovered for 3-4 minutes till the spinach turns tender.
3. Add salt, pepper and stock cube. Mix, add 1 cup water. Give 1-2 boils. Check salt and remove from fire.
4. Serve the soup piping hot with garlic bread.

Mulligatawny : Recipe on page 84 ➤

$\mathscr{N}ita \mathscr{M}ehta's$ BEST SELLERS (Vegetarian)

All Time Favourite
SNACKS

SANDWICHES

Taste of **RAJASTHAN**

Desserts Puddings

ZERO OIL

Delicious Parlour
ICE-CREAMS

Indian Cooking
HANDI TAWA KADHAI

Different ways with
CHAAWAL

PASTA & CORN

PARTY FOOD

PANEER all the way

MENUS from around
the world